GRAY WOLF
RED WOLF

GRAY WOLF
RED WOLF

By DOROTHY HINSHAW PATENT
Photographs by
WILLIAM MUÑOZ

CLARION BOOKS
NEW YORK

For Karin, Neil, and the gang

ACKNOWLEDGMENTS

The author and photographer want to thank Roland Smith, George Garris, Warren Parker, Robert Ream, Mike Fairchild, Diane Boyd, Dale Pedersen, Susan Behrns, John G. Murray, D.V.M., Hank Fisher, Monte Dolack, the Wild Canid Research Center, the U.S. Fish and Wildlife Service, and the Point Defiance Zoo for their help with this book. Thanks also to Bruce and Kelly at Fossil Rim and to the wolves, especially Muff, Denali, and the ugly one from Minnesota.

Clarion Books
a Houghton Mifflin Company imprint
215 Park Avenue South, New York, NY 10003
Text copyright © 1990 by Dorothy Hinshaw Patent
Photographs copyright © 1990 by William Muñoz
All rights reserved.

For information about permission to reproduce selections from this book, write to Permissions, Houghton Mifflin Company, 215 Park Avenue South, New York, NY 10003. Printed in Singapore.

Library of Congress Cataloging-in-Publication Data
Patent, Dorothy Hinshaw.
Gray wolf, red wolf / by Dorothy Hinshaw Patent : photographs by William Muñoz.
p. cm.
Summary: Describes the physical characteristics, life cycle, and behavior of the two species of wolves found in North America and discusses efforts to save them from extinction by reintroducing them to wilderness areas.
ISBN 0-89919-863-5 PA ISBN 0-395-69627-5
1. Wolves — North America — Juvenile literature. 2. Red wolf — North America — Juvenile literature. 3. Wildlife conservation — North America — Juvenile literature. [1. Wolves. 2. Rare animals. 3. Wildlife conservation.] I. Muñoz, William, ill. II. Title.
QL737.C22P38   1990
599.74′442 — dc20   89-77718
CIP AC
TWP 10 9 8 7 6 5 4 3

CONTENTS

1
GRAY WOLVES AND RED WOLVES

Since long before humankind began recording history, the wild howl of wolves resounded across the world's Northern Hemisphere. Europe, most of North America, Japan, and Asia — the gray wolf wandered them all, avoiding only the highest mountains and driest deserts. Because of its ability to survive in so many different areas, the wolf is viewed as one of the most successful hunters ever to live. Gray wolf, eastern timber wolf, tundra wolf, buffalo wolf, arctic wolf — this animal has many names, depending on its homeland. But each is merely a variation of the same species, which scientists refer to as *Canis lupus*.

A typical gray wolf.

Kinds of Wolves

Each of these variations, called *subspecies,* evolved to live in a different habitat. The arctic wolf, for example, lives in the Far North, where there is snow on the ground most months of the year. It has a thick, white coat, and in the wintertime, long fur grows on its legs and between the pads of its feet, which helps protect the arctic wolf from the bitter winter weather.

Wolves look similar to German shepherd and husky dogs, but their legs are longer, their chests are narrower, and their feet are bigger. Wolf tails generally hang down, while dog tails often curl up over their backs. Wolves have a scent gland located on top of their tails that dogs lack.

The name "gray wolf" is confusing, for these animals can be almost any color from pure white to solid black. The coat of most wolves is rich with color — gray, tan, buff, black, and brown hairs making a beautiful pattern of light and dark highlights. The faces of wolves are distinctive, with differing light and dark areas. While many wolves have striking yellow eyes, the eyes of others are amber or dark brown.

Wolves vary considerably in size. The combined length of the head and body usually ranges from forty inches (the size of a small German shepherd) to sixty-three inches (as big as a Saint Bernard). Northern subspecies tend to be larger than southern ones. The smallest in the world is the Arabian wolf, which has a head and body only thirty-two inches long.

Wolves vary greatly in coat color and have distinctive facial markings. Their eyes can range in hue from dark brown to bright yellow.

Thirty-two subspecies of the gray wolf have been recognized by science. While some of these still thrive in the wild, others are extinct, gone forever. A number are seriously endangered. The endangered Mexican wolf, which once roamed southern New Mexico and Arizona as well as a large portion of Mexico, may be extinct in the wild although researchers have seen wolf tracks in remote Mexican areas. In 1988, twenty-eight of them lived in captivity in the United States. Some conservationists are making an effort to reintroduce this magnificent animal into the southwestern states. There are remote areas that would make good homes for it, but getting permission to release wolves into the wild isn't easy.

Finding acceptable homes — that's the problem with large, powerful predators like wolves. Persecution by humans has killed off wolves throughout the lower forty-eight states. Today, only two subspecies survive in the United States outside Alaska — a sizable population of eastern timber wolves in Minnesota with a few scattered animals in northern Michigan and Wisconsin, and some northern Rocky Mountain wolves in northern Montana and Idaho. Most biologists would agree that the wolf is an important, missing element in the natural balance of Yellowstone National Park. Yet the idea of reintroducing it there sets off alarms among ranchers in the area. They fear that the wolves will move out of the park and start preying on their sheep and cattle instead of hunting the abundant Yellowstone elk, deer, and bison.

A Mexican wolf.

Another American Wolf

Before white settlement of America, red wolves ranged from the coasts of Georgia and Florida west to central Texas. They lived along the Mississippi River valley from the Gulf of Mexico north into central Missouri and southern Illinois. In these northern areas, the range of the red wolf, named *Canis rufus* by scientists, overlapped that of the gray wolf. Now, two of the three original subspecies of the red wolf are extinct, the eastern one that lived in Florida and the western one. Only the central subspecies survives.

The red wolf is not actually red. Its color is a blend of cinnamon-brown, black, and gray-brown. Some animals have a reddish cast to their coats, but not all. The red wolf is somewhat smaller than the gray, weighing from fifty-five to eighty pounds.

The red wolf faces many of the same difficulties confronting its gray cousin. Humans took over its habitat, pushing it into undesirable parts of Louisiana and Texas. The red wolf was brought into captivity in the late 1960s to the mid-1970s. By 1980, it was considered to be extinct in the wild, but it was kept alive through captive breeding. In the early 1980s, wildlife biologists developed a proposal to release a few red wolves into the Land Between the Lakes in Tennessee. This area is good red wolf habitat and is relatively isolated from farming areas, but the proposal was turned down by state agencies. Fortunately, other homes have since been found for red wolves.

A red wolf.

Hating Wolves

Humans have a strange relationship with the wolf. When white settlers came to America, the land was inhabited by native Americans living in harmony with wild animals. The Indians hunted for meat and fur. They recognized the importance of each kind of animal in nature's scheme, and they honored the animals in their dances and their stories.

The white settlers came from a different sort of society. They were used to building cities and to taking over the land for growing crops and raising domesticated stock like cattle and sheep. As white settlement spread across North America, wild animals such as the bison were slaughtered to make room for farms, and deer were hunted for meat. With their food reduced and their land taken over, wolves took to feeding on the easiest and most abundant prey available — sheep and cattle.

Starting in the 1600s, the government declared war on wolves and paid a bounty — money for each wolf pelt brought in — so the wolves were hunted down and killed. But they weren't just shot. Many wolves were tortured by their human enemies. They were seen as more than just competitors that attacked animals people wanted for themselves. They were thought of as evil and vicious.

Wolves hunt in order to eat; they have no choice. In a natural situation, wolves rarely kill more than they can use. Occasionally, they may have killed large numbers of penned

Black wolves are especially beautiful.

domesticated animals that couldn't escape, but penned, defenseless animals aren't a part of the natural world wolves live in.

Will wolves attack people? Wolves in Europe may have stalked villagers during desperate winters; we don't know. But in North America, there is no record of a healthy wild wolf attacking a human. On the contrary, wolves are generally very shy and avoid people if at all possible. Captive wolves can become accustomed to humans if they are bottle-fed from before their eyes open and given plenty of exposure to different people while they are young, but even then some never act comfortable around humans.

(Right) *Wolves are bottle-fed to accustom them to humans.*

(Below) *Even when raised by people, captive wolves can be wary of strangers.*

(Facing page) *Wolves eat all the meat they can get from a kill.*

2
WOLVES WILL BE WOLVES

The beautiful black wolf walked toward the others, his tail held high and his ears pricked forward. As he approached, the rest of the pack rose to their feet to greet him. Their tails were lowered and wagging, and their ears slicked back against their heads. They crowded around their leader, licking his face and whining in greeting, jostling one another in their efforts to get as close as possible. After a few minutes, the group broke up and the wolves lay down again quietly, resting before the hunt.

Wolf Society

Like humans, gray wolves are social beings. Their lives are interwoven into a web of cooperation and caring. They hunt together and play together, and the whole pack takes care of the litter of pups born each year. A wolf pack usually begins when a lone male and a lone female find each other and pair

The male wolf (left) *and the female play together before mating.*

up. At first, just the two of them hunt and raise a family. But instead of leaving home, the puppies stay with their parents, and a new pack is formed. Packs can have from three to as many as twenty or even more members.

The wolf pack has a definite structure. At the top is the breeding pair, called the alpha male and the alpha female. These animals are the pack leaders and are "dominant" over the others. That means they mate and produce pups, and they get first choice of food. When they interact with other animals in the pack, the alpha male and female hold their tails high and their ears pricked up. They stand tall, while the other animals crouch down with lowered tails and flattened ears.

During their youthful play, the puppies establish a "pecking order," so named because the system was first seen in chickens. The top pup of each sex is dominant over all the others and is called the beta animal. At the bottom of the heap are the omega male and female, which must behave submissively to all the other pack members.

As the years go by and the wolves get older, the pecking order, also called the hierarchy, in the pack changes. New pups become part of it, and animals may move up and down in the hierarchy, depending on their personalities, hunting skills, and physical strength. An animal lower down in the pecking order may challenge an alpha for pack leadership. If

(Left) A subordinate wolf licks the face of the dominant one. (Right) *When wolf puppies play, they are practicing skills they will need as adults and are also working out their dominance relationships.*

an alpha animal loses, it is likely to go off on its own. If it finds a new mate, it may start a new pack. Omega animals picked on by the others may leave the pack, becoming lone wolves that can travel hundreds of miles to form packs of their own. Now and then, a pack may allow a lone wolf to join.

Having a Family

When wolves approach two years of age, they are old enough to mate. But usually only the alpha female produces pups. She keeps the other females from breeding by dominating them, while the alpha male stops other males from mating. The breeding season occurs sometime from late January through March, depending on where the wolves live. The farther north, the later the breeding season.

If you look closely, you can see a new pup under its mother's belly.

Young wolf pups at play.

The pups are born about sixty-three days after mating, in a den dug into the earth. There are usually five or six pups in a litter. Wolf pups weigh about a pound at birth. Their eyes are closed, and their fur is thin. Their ears flop over, and their muzzles are very short. There is little to distinguish them from dog puppies beyond their wild scent. When they are eleven to fifteen days old, their eyes open. They can worm their way about, exploring the corners of the den. When the pups are about three weeks old, they are allowed to come out of the den and explore the world of sunshine, wildflowers, and rain. They romp about, wrestling and tumbling in play.

Exploring is an important way for young wolves to learn.

The young wolves grow quickly. Their muzzles become long and pointed, and their ears stand straight up. Their fur becomes thick and fluffy underneath, with wiry longer guard hairs. They spend most of their time napping and tussling with one another, building the power and coordination they will need as adults and learning one another's strengths and weaknesses.

During the spring and summer, the whole pack helps care for the pups. All the adult wolves are patient with the puppies, letting them nip at their ears and tails. When the pups are young, the mother stays with them at the den while the rest of the pack hunts for food. After the hunt, the wolves carry extra food in their stomachs back to the den. When the pups lick the hunters' jaws, the adults regurgitate food for them to eat. They also bring food for the mother.

When the young animals are big enough, the den is abandoned. The pups are left at a rendezvous site, an area of about a half acre, while the pack hunts. An adult "baby-sitter," often not the mother, may stay with the youngsters. The first rendezvous site is usually about a mile from the den. As the young wolves grow, the rendezvous site is moved farther and farther away from the den.

By the time the puppies are four to six months of age, they are almost as big as the adults. They are old enough and strong enough to learn how to hunt and join the pack as it wanders in search of game.

(Below left) *Wolf pup about three months old.*
(Below right) *A yearling wolf still doesn't look like an adult.*

Dorothy Hinshaw Patent

How Wolves Hunt

The pack cooperates in hunting, allowing it successfully to bring down big animals like moose. The pack often tests its prey, approaching a herd of deer or caribou to see if one of the animals might be an easy mark. If an individual limps, hangs back from the others, or is a young one with an inattentive mother, it may become wolf food. Wolves will try for the easiest possible prey, which is usually a sick, elderly, or very young animal. At the end of the fall rut, when bull elk fight over the right to mate with the cows, exhausted bulls can be taken down by wolves.

When the wolves find a vulnerable animal, the chase begins. Wolves can run as fast as forty-four miles per hour in a sprint. While one wolf chases, others may lie in wait to take over after the first one tires. This way, fresh wolves can wear out the prey until it is exhausted.

Hunting isn't easy. Wolves are only successful at bringing down prey about once in every ten tries. Prey animals are big and strong, and they have sharp hooves and antlers to protect themselves. Wolves can be injured or even killed as they chase and attack.

After the prey is brought down, the alpha animals feed first, followed by the others. A wolf can eat an amazing amount of food at one time. But if there is more than the animals can consume at once, usually they will return to the kill over a period of days until they have finished it.

Wolves are very well equipped as hunters. Their canine

Rarely are lone wolves successful in hunting large mammals like these Dall sheep in Alaska. Although the wolf is nearby, the sheep seem unconcerned. When the wolf takes chase, the sheep easily escape to the safety of the high rocks and the rest of their band. Sometimes, however, a lone wolf is lucky enough to make a good-sized kill.

teeth—the pointed ones at the front corners of the mouth—can be two inches long. A wolf can hang onto the nose or tail of a fleeing moose with these long, piercing teeth. Farther back in their jaws are large teeth with sharp edges for cutting through tough skin and muscle.

Wolves have very sensitive noses. They can detect prey from a mile and a half away using their sense of smell. Compared with a wolf's, our sense of smell is pitiful. While the sense cells inside our noses that can detect odors cover an area about the size of a postage stamp, those of a wolf are spread over a region as big as a bandana. Not only can wolves detect odors that are faint or nonexistent to us, they can distinguish an amazing variety of scents.

Wolves have an excellent sense of smell that they rely on strongly.

Wolf Territories

Each wolf pack has its own territory, an area within which it lives, dens, and hunts. Territories vary in size, depending on the abundance of food. Where game is plentiful, a territory may be 25 square miles in size. But where hunting is chancier, such as in central Canada, territories can be as large as 540 square miles. Around the edges of the territories are areas where both packs may enter briefly. But if a wolf strays into the territory of another pack, it risks death if the other wolves are nearby. Hungry packs have been seen giving up the chase when deer cross a boundary.

How do wolves know where the territory of another pack begins? The boundaries are clearly marked by urine. The pack members, especially the alpha male and female, urinate on bushes, rocks, and trees around the territory edges, leaving clear scent marks showing where the boundaries are. The marks are renewed periodically.

Wolf Communication

The most spectacular way wolves "talk" to one another is by howling. A pack can tell if a neighboring pack is too close to the boundary when it hears them howl. Wolves often howl together before a hunt or after successfully bringing down game. When one wolf is separated from the pack, it may howl to indicate its location to the others, and they may howl back to show where they are.

The howl of the wolf is a powerful sound, and each voice

is different, just as with humans. When wolves howl together, they sing on a variety of notes, making a chorus that sounds like more animals than are really present. People in wolf country can sometimes get wolves to howl back by giving out their own version of the howl.

Wolves have other ways of communicating as well. We've already learned about scent marking and body postures that show dominance and submission. But wolves also use other sounds besides the howl. Like dogs, they growl in threat or bark in warning, although wolves don't bark very often. Whining shows submission or the need for attention.

(Far left) *The howl of the wolf is an eerie and beautiful sound.*
(Below) *The wolf on its side is showing submission to the wolf above it. Notice that its ears are back and its tail is tucked in.*

3
RETURN OF THE RED WOLF

The male and female red wolves paced back and forth in their pen as the humans approached. Although they had spent their entire lives in captivity, they had never lost their fear of people. That was as it should be, for these animals were soon to become among the first red wolves to live free in more than twenty years.

After entering the pen, the wildlife biologists chased the wolf pair into a small side cage. Then they began the hunt for the two pups, hidden somewhere in the doghouse or the tunnels the animals had dug beneath it. One pup was found right away, cowering silently in the house. He gave no resistance and was picked up carefully by the scruff of the neck and placed in a carrying cage. His brother was harder to find, as he hid motionlessly at the end of one of the burrows.

(Above left) *Julius Loflin pulls a pup from a burrow while George Garris, manager of Cape Romain National Wildlife Refuge, looks on.* (Above right) *Julius reassures the pup.*

Once both pups were captured, the humans released the parents back into the pen and took the pups on a long adventure. They bounced along the rutted road in the back of a truck to the waiting boat, which took them from Bull's Island, part of the Cape Romain National Wildlife Refuge, to the South Carolina mainland. There, they waited together in their cage until the next morning, when a truck carried them to the office of a veterinarian in nearby Charleston.

As the vet lifted the first pup from his cage, the animal's intelligent gray-green eyes showed fear, and his large, sensitive ears were folded back along his neck. How could he know that what was going to happen was for his own good and for the good of his kind? The pup and his family were bound for freedom. The door to their pen would be opened, and they would be able to roam wherever they wanted through the thick woods of Bull's Island.

(Below left) *A boat takes them to a clinic on the mainland.* (Below right) *Veterinarian Dr. John Murray checks a pup to make sure it is healthy.*

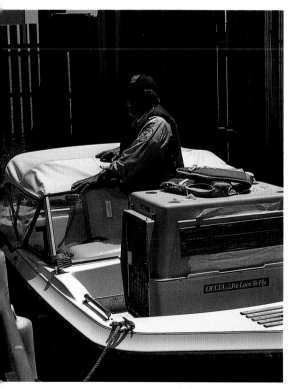

But the scientists needed to know where the animals were, in case they got into trouble. The adults already sported special collars, fitted with small radio transmitters that gave off beeps. The beeps could be picked up by hand-carried receivers, so the location of the animals could be checked as often as necessary. These radio collars, however, are not practical for pups. Because the animals grow so quickly, collars would need repeated readjustment, and the pups would have to be trapped over and over again.

So, instead of putting the radio transmitter on the outside of the animal, it was put inside. After the pup was anesthetized, the vet made a small slit in its abdomen and slipped

(Below left) *The radio transmitter that goes into the pup's body cavity.*
(Below right) *A pup recovers after surgery.*

a sausage-shaped radio transmitter inside. Then the cut was sewn up, and the second pup received the same treatment.

This technique sounds alarming, but it rarely results in complications. Scientists had used it for years on other species such as coyotes. The transmitter settles inside the body cavity and causes no disturbance to the animal.

After surgery, the pups were hurried back to their pen on Bull's Island. They had been away from their parents for a long time and had undergone some frightening experiences. But they readjusted quickly, as young animals will do. And within a few days, the door of their cage was opened and the wolf family was able to taste the freedom natural to its kind.

The pups are returned to their parents. After they have completely recovered from surgery, the door to the pen is opened, and the wolves are free to go.

Decline of the Red Wolf

The decline of the red wolf began early, since the southeast was an area of early colonization by both Spanish and northern European settlers. The woods that harbored the red wolf were cut down, and the marshes where it roamed were drained. The wolf was hunted for its fur and because it was considered a danger to livestock. The red wolf's home had been turned into the drier, more open country preferred by coyotes. Coyotes moved in from the north and west. Before the disturbances of human settlement, coyotes and red wolves didn't normally interbreed. But the few remaining red wolves had difficulty finding mates, so crossing with the more abundant coyote became common. Once the hybrids were produced, they multiplied and took over more and more of the red wolf's habitat.

The red wolf was recognized as an endangered species in 1967. Not much was done about it, however, until after the Endangered Species Act was passed in 1973. That legislation focused efforts on keeping plants and animals from going extinct. Meanwhile, the red wolf–coyote hybrids were spreading farther and farther south. Some red wolves were already in captivity, but biologists worried that coyotes would overwhelm the few pure red wolves remaining along the Gulf coast. In 1975, the U.S. Fish and Wildlife Service took action. About four hundred animals were captured from the area. Many of them were in very bad health, forced by people to live in the subtropical wetlands, where they contracted

The red wolf (above) *is bigger than the coyote* (below).

heartworm and mange from nearby dogs and other wild animals such as raccoons and coyotes.

After careful examination, forty of the animals were sent to Graham, Washington, where mink-farm owner Dale Pedersen provided a portion of his land as a refuge for the wolves. The animals were carefully studied. Their blood was analyzed, and they were bred with one another to see if any coyotelike offspring resulted. When the testing was all over, only fourteen of the animals turned out to be pure red wolves. The rescue had happened just in time.

Mystery of the Red Wolf

Unfortunately, we know almost nothing about the natural behavior of red wolves in the wild, since they became scarce so early in the century. Scientists believe that red wolves don't form packs like gray wolves. The mother and father both care for the pups, which then leave their parents the next year. But there are old reports of packs of wolves in the South, so maybe they do sometimes form larger groups.

Red wolves eat whatever comes along that they can catch. They feed on raccoons, rabbits, rats, and muskrats. They may occasionally kill young deer. No one knows for sure if red wolves would cause problems for farmers and ranchers. But chickens, goats, and young sheep might become victims when red wolves are allowed to roam free. Management plans must take this possibility into account.

A pair of red wolves with one of their pups.

The mother red wolf takes good care of her puppies.

Eventually, when enough red wolves live in the wild that they can be left alone to develop their natural social order, we may learn more about their way of life. But over the next decade, the important thing will be to return the red wolf to its home and help it become wild again.

Red Wolf Recovery

Fortunately, red wolves breed readily in captivity. During some years, females were given hormones to keep them from getting pregnant. Not enough zoos were interested in having the animals, and there was no point in increasing the

Researcher Evan Blumer examines a very young red wolf pup.

population if there were no homes for the young wolves. Things began to change, however, in 1986, when red wolves were reintroduced into the Alligator River National Wildlife Refuge in North Carolina. Before then, no one knew if animals that had spent their entire lives in captivity could survive in the wild. But survive they did, and the word began to spread. The first introduction of a captive-born and captive-bred species into the wild was a success. Conservationists, the media, and the government showed more interest.

As of early 1990, the future of the red wolf looked bright. The pups released on Bull's Island thrived despite the fact that their mother was killed, apparently by an alligator. The two youngsters were taken to Alligator River and released. Later, one was killed by a car. Their father was given a new mate in early 1989, and the two of them produced a litter of five pups. The female and one pup died. Then hurricane Hugo hit, its huge waves and high winds breaking off every tree on the island at the ten-foot level. But miraculously, the wolves survived. The male, however, died three weeks later. By then, the pups were old enough to make it on their own.

Another red wolf pair living in a pen on Horn Island off the Mississippi coast had seven pups. The family was released that summer. The adult female died late in the summer, but her mate stayed with the puppies and took care of them. Two females at Alligator River that had lived successfully in the wild were brought in for breeding. They and their families will also be released. In addition, two female pups born at Alligator River in 1988 are still in the wild. A pair of red wolves was placed in a den on St. Vincent Island off the Gulf coast of Florida. In the summer of 1990, the pair and their pups will be released to live free on the island. Altogether, there were twenty-seven red wolves in the wild in early 1990, with more to come.

The goal of the Red Wolf Recovery Plan is to have around 225 animals in the wild and 330 in captivity. The captive-breeding program should meet its goal within five to ten years. But it will take longer to get 225 red wolves living in the wild. The dedication of the biologists involved and the toughness of this wilderness survivor make success likely.

(Above) *A pup just ready to be released into the wild with its parents.* (Below) *Even as a young baby, the red wolf shows its wild nature by baring its teeth at humans.*

4

WOLVES IN NORTH AMERICA TODAY

Gray wolves once roamed over most of the North American continent, except in coastal areas of southern California, in the hottest deserts, and in the deep southeast. While only a few populations now live south of the Canadian border, wolves still wander most of the wilderness in Alaska and Canada. In those areas, wolves are not endangered and can be hunted.

Wolves are hunted for two reasons. Their beautiful fur is used for coats and rugs, but its best use is as trim around the edges of parkas, jackets worn in the north. Wolf fur doesn't hold frost the way most fur does, so the breath of a person wearing a wolf fur–trimmed parka won't form crystals around the edge of the hood. The other reason wolves are hunted is to keep game populations high for human hunters.

Big-game hunting brings millions of dollars into the economy of Canadian provinces and Alaska. Many hunters believe that wolves compete with them for game, but scientists aren't sure if this is so.

Still, the question of wolf hunting is far from settled in either Alaska or Canada. While big-game hunters worry that wolves will leave less game available, many nonhunters object strongly to hunting wolves. The two sides battle often in court and in legislatures. Whether wolves can be hunted from airplanes is especially controversial. Airplane hunting is not presently allowed in Alaska but still goes on in some parts of Canada. While bounties for wolves have been abandoned in the United States, wolf hunters can still collect them in certain areas of Canada.

Americans are especially concerned about hunting in southern British Columbia, which lies just north of Glacier National Park, an area where wolves are slowly coming back to the United States. The wolves know no boundaries, traveling freely across the border. If they go into Canada during the hunting season, they risk death. In past years, wolves that grew up in Glacier have been killed by the guns of Canadian hunters.

Wolves are viewed as competitors with human hunters where they are still abundant, but they are officially endangered in forty-seven of the lower forty-eight states. Endangered species are protected from hunting. In Minnesota, wolves are classified as "threatened," and some people believe hunting them should be allowed.

This wolf is lucky — it lives in Denali National Park in Alaska, where it is protected from hunting.

Wolves in Minnesota

Minnesota is the only place in the United States other than Alaska where wolves thrive today, and they manage to do so even in cattle country. More than a thousand wolves roam the northeastern part of the state today. But during the 1960s, hunting and trapping of wolves were taking their toll in Minnesota, and environmentalists went into action. In 1965, the bounty on wolves was stopped, and in 1970, the Superior National Forest was closed to wolf hunting. Wolves finally had a safe place to roam and hunt in the United States.

Since then, protection from hunting has been extended to all wolves in Minnesota. However, illegal killing is quite common. For example, in early 1989, seven of sixteen wolves

Because many people feel a special attraction to wolves, they oppose wolf hunting.

A Minnesota wolf.

equipped with radio collars in Voyageurs National Park on the Canadian border were killed. Many more wolves that can't be so easily traced have also died. Some estimate that as many as a third of all wolves in Minnesota are illegally killed each year. Deer hunters lure them with the guts from deer they shoot, and coyote trappers get them in their traps.

The Minnesota wolves coexist with about 234,000 head of cattle and 91,000 sheep. Wolves do kill some livestock — around 12 sheep and 5 head of cattle for every 10,000 on the range. But the state government pays ranchers for losses to the wolves. Although some ranchers are not happy about the wolves, wolf recovery in Minnesota has worked well, with relatively little negative impact on people.

The Wolves of Isle Royale

Isle Royale National Park lies far north, an island in Lake Superior between northern Michigan and Minnesota. Isle Royale is a special place. Its 210 square miles are without roads, and human visitors can venture there for only six and a half months out of twelve. Wolves have lived there since 1949, when an especially severe winter allowed an ice bridge to form between the island and the mainland. The island moose population at that time had no predators, so there was

Moose are the staple food of wolves on Isle Royale.

plenty of prey for the wolves to hunt. Moose and wolf formed a partnership. The moose provided the wolves with food, and the wolves kept the moose from overpopulating the island and bringing on a disastrous population crash like the one they had faced during the 1930s. At that time, there were over two thousand moose, and they starved in huge numbers one winter. Only a few hundred moose survived, and the whole island reeked from the smell of dead animals.

Scientists have studied the Isle Royale wolves and moose for more than thirty years, documenting the ancient relationship between the predators and their prey. From 1949 to the late 1970s, the balance between the two species remained good. But as wolf numbers climbed, the moose population fell. Fewer and fewer young, weak, or old moose were available for the wolves to hunt. In 1980, the wolf population reached an all-time high of fifty animals. Then, within two years, only fourteen wolves were left. As scientists expected, the moose population began to increase again, free from the hunting pressure of so many wolves. By 1984, the wolves had recovered to twenty-four, which had been their average number before their big rise.

Then a strange thing happened. During the winter of 1987–88, the wolves began dying again, leaving only about a dozen. Until this time, the animals had been studied from a distance, largely from small planes. When the scientists did descend to the ground, it was to examine moose carcasses and wolf scat, not to trap and radio-collar the wolves.

Unfortunately, this comfortable relationship ended in

1988. The scientists feared that all the wolves might die off without their knowing why. So in the summer of 1988, four wolves were trapped on the island. Their blood was sampled, and they were fitted with radio collars. The collars made it easier to track the wolves and would give off a special signal if the animal didn't move for a few hours, so the scientists would know if it had died.

The animals' blood could hold clues to why so many wolves had died. The most likely culprit is parvovirus, a disease that kills dogs and wolves. There was an epidemic of parvo in 1981 in Houghton, Michigan, one of two towns from which visitors take boats to the island. Perhaps parvo helped cause the original wolf decline, along with the reduction in the number of moose. Visitors to Isle Royale aren't allowed to bring pets along, but some do anyway. Two of the four wolves did have antibodies to parvo in their bloodstreams, indicating that they had been exposed to the disease.

Another possible cause of the wolves' decline is inbreeding. It's possible that only one pair of wolves crossed the ice bridge to Isle Royale in 1949. If so, all the wolves there would be very closely related and thus could be susceptible to a number of problems caused by inbreeding. Scientists are testing the blood to see just how inbred the wolves are in comparison with other wolf populations. In 1989, the wolves produced a litter of pups, so there is hope again for their recovery. But even if the Isle Royale wolves disappear completely, studying them will have taught us a great deal about wild wolves and the problems they can face.

Rocky Mountain Recovery

While Minnesota has a healthy wolf population, wolves are just beginning to repopulate the Rockies in the northern United States. It started in 1979, when tracks of a lone wolf were found. Then, in 1982, a researcher stumbled upon a litter of seven puppies waiting for their parents at a rendez-vous site in Canada, just north of Glacier National Park.

Wolves will mate with their brothers or sisters, like this pair.

Glacier National Park.

Altogether, about two dozen wolves live in two or three packs in northwestern Montana. Their numbers vary from year to year. For example, the first certain denning in Montana was recorded in 1985. By 1987, three packs were denning in the park. But that fall, six of seven animals in one pack were killed during the British Columbia wolf hunt, and the numbers of animals in Glacier have dropped since then. In 1989, only one pack was in the park, and both its pups died from unknown causes. Fortunately, the wolf hunt in southeastern British Columbia was canceled that year, giving the Glacier wolves a better chance to recover.

Meanwhile, wolves continue to move into the country from Canada. In 1989, a pack denned west of Glacier, near Marion, Montana. The alpha male and female and two of their pups were trapped and relocated into the park for safety. Unfortunately, the family then split up, and the abandoned pups starved to death. The male wolf died because his foot became infected from the trap, and the female wandered far south, away from the protection of the park.

Researcher Diane Boyd carefully sets a trap as part of the ongoing study of the wolf's return to Montana. Trapped wolves are fitted with radio collars so they can be tracked by scientists.

Wolves in Yellowstone?

Wolves are a natural part of life in Yellowstone National Park, but they have been absent since the 1920s, when they were hunted and trapped as enemies of the deer and elk that visitors wanted to see. Since then, biologists have come to understand that predators are necessary to maintain healthy populations of prey animals. Like the moose in Isle Royale, the populations of elk in Yellowstone kept growing without predators. As their food became more and more scarce, the elk fed on young pine trees, damaging their future growth. They ate pine bark, too, weakening the mature trees. But the winter of 1988–89 was severe, and many elk died of starvation. Overpopulation took its toll.

When wolves are reintroduced into Yellowstone National Park, elk will be one of their main sources of food.

RESTORING THE WOLF TO
YELLOWSTONE NATIONAL PARK
DEFENDERS OF WILDLIFE

Artist Monte Dolack created this poster to help the Defenders of Wildlife's efforts to return wolves to the park. Proceeds from this poster will reimburse ranchers for livestock lost to wolves.

If wolves come back to Yellowstone, elk populations should remain more constant. The wolves may also prey upon bison calves; bison, like the elk, have become overpopulated in the park. But bringing wolves back won't be easy. Even though park visitors overwhelmingly support the return of the wolf, ranchers who graze their stock around the park boundaries are worried. They fear the wolves will wander from the park and attack their herds. As an endangered species, wolves can't be shot when they attack livestock, so ranchers might be helpless to protect their animals. Conservationists, politicians, and ranchers are trying to work out compromises that will protect livestock while allowing the wolf to take its proper place in the natural ecosystem in Yellowstone National Park.

Wildlife biologists hope that Mexican wolves like this one will soon find a home in the wild.

Before any wolves could be transplanted to the park, an environmental impact statement must be prepared. This study would explore all aspects of wolf reintroduction—effects on park elk, deer, and bison; growth of the wolf population; risks to livestock near the park; and so forth. In 1989, a bill introduced into Congress called for the preparation of the environmental impact statement.

The Mexican Wolf

While wolves have been moving themselves into the United States from Canada, environmentalists have been frustrated in their efforts to find a home for the endangered Mexican wolf. This animal once roamed the mountains of Mexico and north into southwestern New Mexico, southeastern Arizona, and western Texas. Starting in 1914, the Mexican wolf was persecuted just like the other subspecies. By the early 1920s, only a few were left in the United States. Ranchers wouldn't be happy until all the wolves were gone, and the last one in Arizona died in 1960, the last in Texas in 1970, and the final holdout in New Mexico in 1976. Ironically, the Mexican wolf was placed on the endangered species list that same year.

In 1977, the recovery project began with two males and one pregnant female brought in from Mexico. Since then, Mexican wolves have been bred in captivity, with hopes that they can eventually be released back into their rightful home, the wilds of the Southwest. Unfortunately, finding places where they are welcome is difficult, just as it has been for wolves elsewhere. Conservationists must continue to work with ranchers to solve problems involved in wolf reintroduction so that wolves can again live freely where they belong.

INDEX

Page numbers in *italics* refer to illustrations.

SELECTED LIST OF ADDRESSES FOR WOLF INFORMATION

CANADIAN WOLF DEFENDERS
P.O. Box 3480 Station D
Edmonton, Alberta, Canada T5L 4J3
Dedicated to the preservation of wolves on wilderness lands.

DEFENDERS OF WILDLIFE
1244 19th St. NW
Washington, D.C. 20036
Dedicated to the preservation of wildlife, with wolf reintroduction a special interest.

H.O.W.L. (Help Our Wolves Live)
4600 Emerson Ave. South
Minneapolis, MN 55409
Committee for protection of the wolf.

INTERNATIONAL WOLF CENTER
c/o Vermilion Community College
1900 E. Camp St.
Ely, MN 55731
Home for the Wolves & Humans exhibit, world's largest wolf educational center.

MEXICAN WOLF COALITION
2825 Candelaria NW
Albuquerque, NM 87107
Dedicated to the reintroduction of the Mexican gray wolf in New Mexico.

NATIONAL WILDLIFE FEDERATION
8925 Leesburg Pike
Vienna, VA 22184
Wildlife conservation organization, with wolves and wolf reintroduction among its interests.

P.A.W.S.
Preserve Arizona's Wolves
1413 E. Dobbins Rd. Phoenix, AZ 85040
Dedicated to the preservation and reintroduction of the Mexican gray wolf in the Southwest.

TIMBERWOLF ALLIANCE
c/o Sigurd Olson Institute
Northland College
Ashland, WI 54806-3999
Coalition of organizations dedicated to educating the public about wolves.

WILD CANID SURVIVAL & RESEARCH CENTER
Wolf Sanctuary, P.O. Box 760
Eureka, MO 63025
Captive breeding facility for endangered red and Mexican wolves.

WOLF AWARENESS INC.
G-2 Farms, RR 3
Ailsa Craig, Ontario
Canada N0M 1A0
Wild wolf study group.

THE WOLF FUND
P.O. Box 471
Moose, WY 83012
Promotes wolf recovery in Yellowstone National Park.

WOLF HAVEN
3111 Offut Lake Rd.
Tenino, WA 98589
Dedicated to the protection of wild wolves and home to unwanted captive wolves.

WOLF PARK
No. Am. Wildlife Park Foundation
Battle Ground, IN 47920
Wildlife preserve.

WOLVES AND RELATED CANIDS
P.O. Box 1026
Agoura, CA 91301
Magazine dealing with wolves, their relatives, and captive wolf hybrids.